OUR FAMILY HISTORY

A Genealogy Workbook

CONTENTS

Ancestral History

Knowing, recording, and preserving your family history directly impacts you, your family, and even future generations of people you may never know. We trying to help make that possible with this Genealogy Organizer!

This Workbook offers users a template featuring multiple trees fan chart views, timeline and mapping, record hints, and research help!

Record the history of ancestors helps gain a greater understanding of the challenges they faced, and it often inspires greater respect, love, and compassion.

Ancestors history is more than names and genealogy. It is about people who lived and had lives like ours.

**Get Start Step-by-Step
to Build Your Family Ancestors History with Love and Proud!**

FIVE GENERATION PEDIGREE CHART

Compiled By: _____

Date: _____

PATERNAL GRANDFATHER

Name

Birth Date

Birth Place

Death Date

Death Place

Marriage Date

Marriage Place

PATERNAL GRANDMOTHER

Name

Birth Date

Birth Place

Death Date

Death Place

YOUR FATHER

Name

Birth Date

Birth Place

Death Date

Death Place

Marriage Date

Marriage Place

YOU

Name

Birth Date

Birth Place

Marriage Date

Marriage Place

MATERNAL GRANDFATHER

Name

Birth Date

Birth Place

Death Date

Death Place

Marriage Date

Marriage Place

YOUR MOTHER

Name

Birth Date

Birth Place

Death Date

Death Place

MATERNAL GRANDFATHER

Name

Birth Date

Birth Place

Death Date

Death Place

PATERNAL GREAT-GRANDFATHER

Name

Birth Date/Place

Death Date/Place

PATERNAL GREAT-GRANDMOTHER

Name

Birth Date/Place

Death Date/Place

PATERNAL GREAT-GRANDFATHER

Name

Birth Date/Place

Death Date/Place

PATERNAL GREAT-GRANDMOTHER

Name

Birth Date/Place

Death Date/Place

MATERNAL GREAT- GRANDFATHER

Name

Birth Date/Place

Death Date/Place

MATERNAL GREAT-GRANDMOTHER

Name

Birth Date/Place

Death Date/Place

MATERNAL GREAT- GRANDFATHER

Name

Birth Date/Place

Death Date/Place

MATERNAL GREAT- GRANDFATHER

Name

Birth Date/Place

Death Date/Place

PATERNAL GREAT-GREAT-GRANDFATHER
Name

Birth Date
Death Date

PATERNAL GREAT-GREAT-GRANDMOTHER
Name

Birth Date
Death Date

PATERNAL GREAT-GREAT-GRANDFATHER
Name

Birth Date
Death Date

PATERNAL GREAT-GREAT-GRANDMOTHER
Name

Birth Date
Death Date

PATERNAL GREAT-GREAT-GRANDFATHER
Name

Birth Date
Death Date

PATERNAL GREAT-GREAT-GRANDMOTHER
Name

Birth Date
Death Date

PATERNAL GREAT-GREAT-GRANDFATHER
Name

Birth Date
Death Date

PATERNAL GREAT-GREAT-GRANDMOTHER
Name

Birth Date
Death Date

MATERNAL GREAT-GREAT-GRANDFATHER
Name

Birth Date
Death Date

MATERNAL GREAT-GREAT-GRANDMOTHER
Name

Birth Date
Death Date

MATERNAL GREAT-GREAT-GRANDFATHER
Name

Birth Date
Death Date

MATERNAL GREAT-GREAT-GRANDMOTHER
Name

Birth Date
Death Date

MATERNAL GREAT-GREAT-GRANDFATHER
Name

Birth Date
Death Date

MATERNAL GREAT-GREAT-GRANDMOTHER
Name

Birth Date
Death Date

MATERNAL GREAT-GREAT-GRANDFATHER
Name

Birth Date
Death Date

MATERNAL GREAT-GREAT-GRANDMOTHER
Name

Birth Date
Death Date

BIRTH COUNTRY

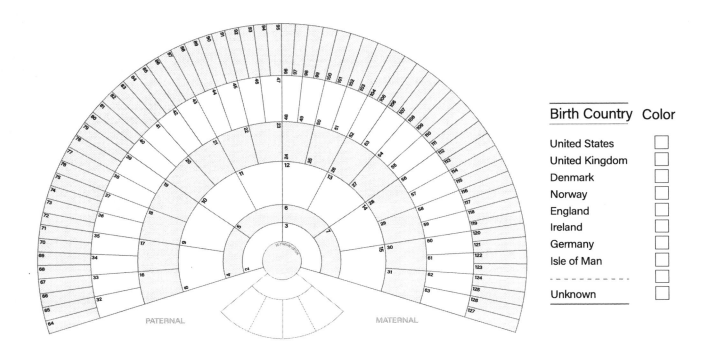

Birth Country   Color

United States

United Kingdom

Denmark

Norway

England

Ireland

Germany

Isle of Man

Unknown

PATERNAL   MATERNAL

The Birth Country FAN CHART is a perfect way to see
what countries you and your family come from.

Color each box based on where your ancestors were born.

BIRTH COUNTRY

Compiled By: _____

Date: _____

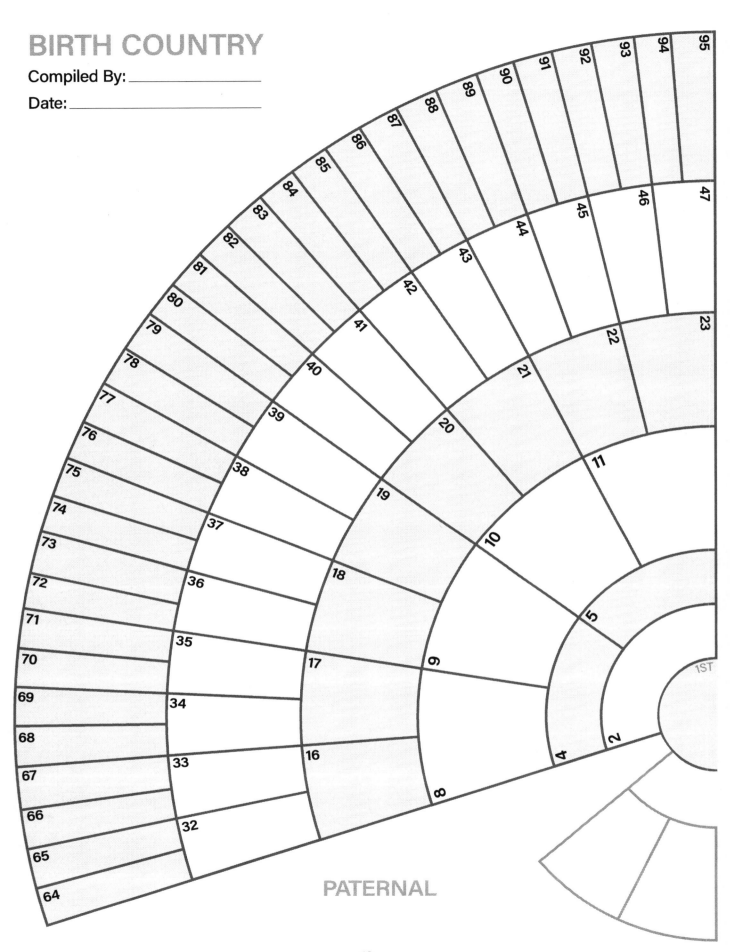

PATERNAL

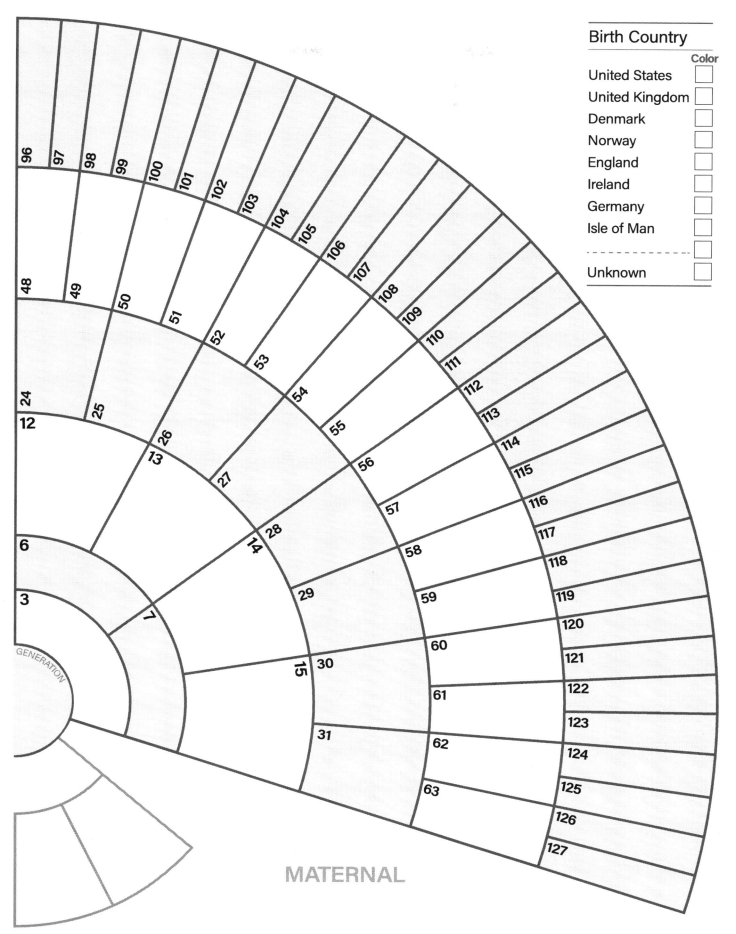

GENERATION

MATERNAL

SOURCES

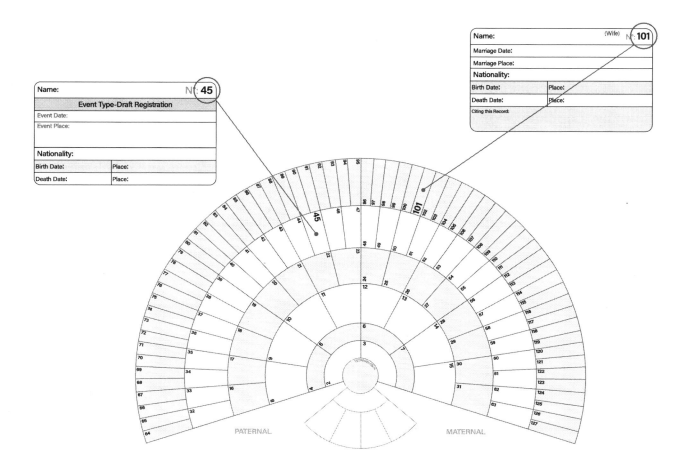

The Sources view clarification each box in the FAN CHART according to how many sources are attached to the person.

This view can especially help you discover people in your family tree who could use a few more sources.

SOURCES

Compiled By: _____

Date: _____

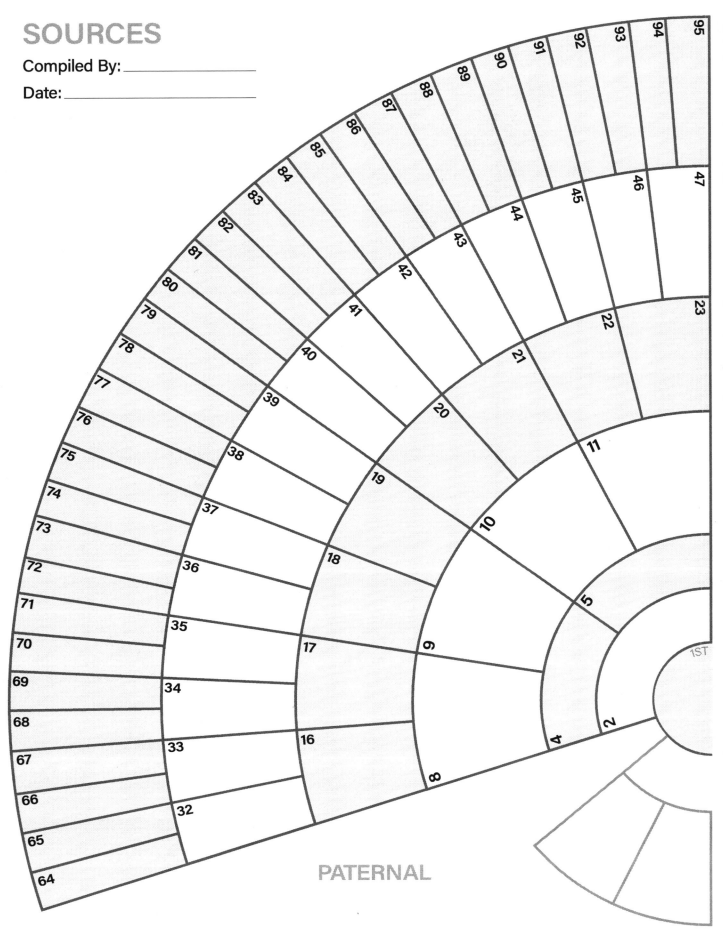

PATERNAL

1ST

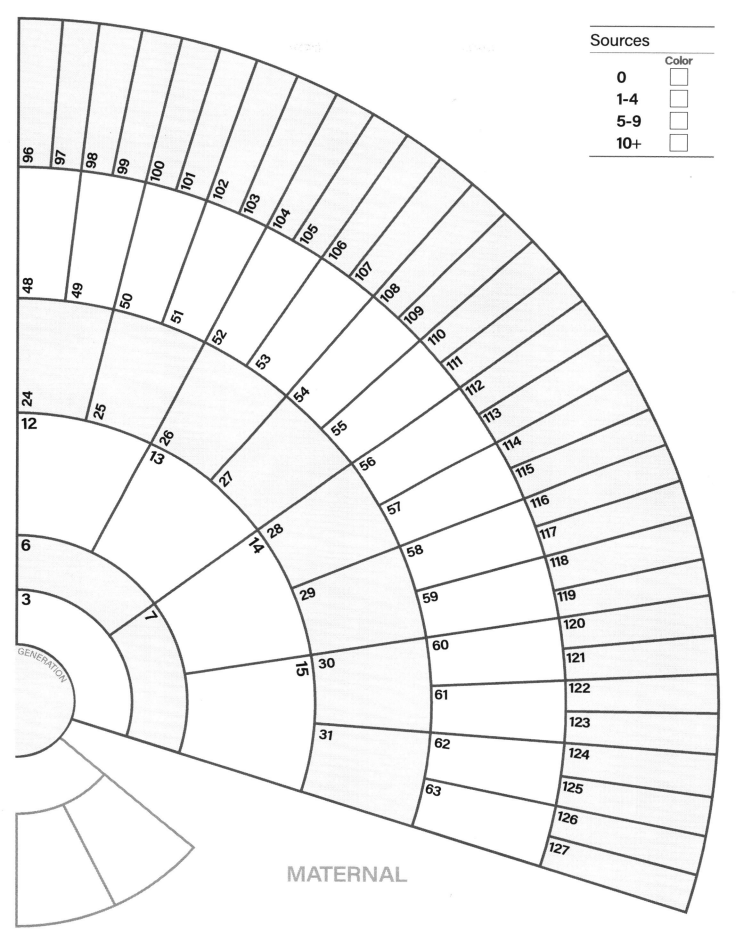

Sources

	Color
0	☐
1-4	☐
5-9	☐
10+	☐

GENERATION

MATERNAL

SOURCES

Name: N°:

Event Type-Draft Registration	
Event Date:	
Event Place:	
Nationality:	
Birth Date:	Place:
Death Date:	Place:

Name: (Wife)   N°:

Marriage Date:	
Marriage Place:	
Nationality:	
Birth Date:	Place:
Death Date:	Place:
Citing this Record:	

Name: N°:

Event Type-Draft Registration	
Event Date:	
Event Place:	
Nationality:	
Birth Date:	Place:
Death Date:	Place:

Name: (Wife)   N°:

Marriage Date:	
Marriage Place:	
Nationality:	
Birth Date:	Place:
Death Date:	Place:
Citing this Record:	

Name: N°:

Event Type-Draft Registration	
Event Date:	
Event Place:	
Nationality:	
Birth Date:	Place:
Death Date:	Place:

Name: (Wife)   N°:

Marriage Date:	
Marriage Place:	
Nationality:	
Birth Date:	Place:
Death Date:	Place:
Citing this Record:	

Name: N°:

Event Type-Draft Registration	
Event Date:	
Event Place:	
Nationality:	
Birth Date:	Place:
Death Date:	Place:

Name: (Wife)   N°:

Marriage Date:	
Marriage Place:	
Nationality:	
Birth Date:	Place:
Death Date:	Place:
Citing this Record:	

SOURCES

Name:	N°:
Event Type-Draft Registration	
Event Date:	
Event Place:	
Nationality:	
Birth Date:	Place:
Death Date:	Place:

Name:	(Wife) N°:
Marriage Date:	
Marriage Place:	
Nationality:	
Birth Date:	Place:
Death Date:	Place:
Citing this Record:	

Name:	N°:
Event Type-Draft Registration	
Event Date:	
Event Place:	
Nationality:	
Birth Date:	Place:
Death Date:	Place:

Name:	(Wife) N°:
Marriage Date:	
Marriage Place:	
Nationality:	
Birth Date:	Place:
Death Date:	Place:
Citing this Record:	

Name:	N°:
Event Type-Draft Registration	
Event Date:	
Event Place:	
Nationality:	
Birth Date:	Place:
Death Date:	Place:

Name:	(Wife) N°:
Marriage Date:	
Marriage Place:	
Nationality:	
Birth Date:	Place:
Death Date:	Place:
Citing this Record:	

Name:	N°:
Event Type-Draft Registration	
Event Date:	
Event Place:	
Nationality:	
Birth Date:	Place:
Death Date:	Place:

Name:	(Wife) N°:
Marriage Date:	
Marriage Place:	
Nationality:	
Birth Date:	Place:
Death Date:	Place:
Citing this Record:	

SOURCES

Name:	N°:
Event Type-Draft Registration	
Event Date:	
Event Place:	
Nationality:	
Birth Date:	Place:
Death Date:	Place:

Name:	(Wife) N°:
Marriage Date:	
Marriage Place:	
Nationality:	
Birth Date:	Place:
Death Date:	Place:
Citing this Record:	

Name:	N°:
Event Type-Draft Registration	
Event Date:	
Event Place:	
Nationality:	
Birth Date:	Place:
Death Date:	Place:

Name:	(Wife) N°:
Marriage Date:	
Marriage Place:	
Nationality:	
Birth Date:	Place:
Death Date:	Place:
Citing this Record:	

Name:	N°:
Event Type-Draft Registration	
Event Date:	
Event Place:	
Nationality:	
Birth Date:	Place:
Death Date:	Place:

Name:	(Wife) N°:
Marriage Date:	
Marriage Place:	
Nationality:	
Birth Date:	Place:
Death Date:	Place:
Citing this Record:	

Name:	N°:
Event Type-Draft Registration	
Event Date:	
Event Place:	
Nationality:	
Birth Date:	Place:
Death Date:	Place:

Name:	(Wife) N°:
Marriage Date:	
Marriage Place:	
Nationality:	
Birth Date:	Place:
Death Date:	Place:
Citing this Record:	

SOURCES

Name:	N°:

Event Type-Draft Registration	
Event Date:	
Event Place:	
Nationality:	
Birth Date:	Place:
Death Date:	Place:

Name:	(Wife) N°:
Marriage Date:	
Marriage Place:	
Nationality:	
Birth Date:	Place:
Death Date:	Place:
Citing this Record:	

Name:	N°:

Event Type-Draft Registration	
Event Date:	
Event Place:	
Nationality:	
Birth Date:	Place:
Death Date:	Place:

Name:	(Wife) N°:
Marriage Date:	
Marriage Place:	
Nationality:	
Birth Date:	Place:
Death Date:	Place:
Citing this Record:	

Name:	N°:

Event Type-Draft Registration	
Event Date:	
Event Place:	
Nationality:	
Birth Date:	Place:
Death Date:	Place:

Name:	(Wife) N°:
Marriage Date:	
Marriage Place:	
Nationality:	
Birth Date:	Place:
Death Date:	Place:
Citing this Record:	

Name:	N°:

Event Type-Draft Registration	
Event Date:	
Event Place:	
Nationality:	
Birth Date:	Place:
Death Date:	Place:

Name:	(Wife) N°:
Marriage Date:	
Marriage Place:	
Nationality:	
Birth Date:	Place:
Death Date:	Place:
Citing this Record:	

SOURCES

Name:	N°:
Event Type-Draft Registration	
Event Date:	
Event Place:	
Nationality:	
Birth Date:	Place:
Death Date:	Place:

Name:	(Wife) N°:
Marriage Date:	
Marriage Place:	
Nationality:	
Birth Date:	Place:
Death Date:	Place:
Citing this Record:	

Name:	N°:
Event Type-Draft Registration	
Event Date:	
Event Place:	
Nationality:	
Birth Date:	Place:
Death Date:	Place:

Name:	(Wife) N°:
Marriage Date:	
Marriage Place:	
Nationality:	
Birth Date:	Place:
Death Date:	Place:
Citing this Record:	

Name:	N°:
Event Type-Draft Registration	
Event Date:	
Event Place:	
Nationality:	
Birth Date:	Place:
Death Date:	Place:

Name:	(Wife) N°:
Marriage Date:	
Marriage Place:	
Nationality:	
Birth Date:	Place:
Death Date:	Place:
Citing this Record:	

Name:	N°:
Event Type-Draft Registration	
Event Date:	
Event Place:	
Nationality:	
Birth Date:	Place:
Death Date:	Place:

Name:	(Wife) N°:
Marriage Date:	
Marriage Place:	
Nationality:	
Birth Date:	Place:
Death Date:	Place:
Citing this Record:	

SOURCES

Name:	N°:
Event Type-Draft Registration	
Event Date:	
Event Place:	
Nationality:	
Birth Date:	Place:
Death Date:	Place:

Name:	(Wife) N°:
Marriage Date:	
Marriage Place:	
Nationality:	
Birth Date:	Place:
Death Date:	Place:
Citing this Record:	

Name:	N°:
Event Type-Draft Registration	
Event Date:	
Event Place:	
Nationality:	
Birth Date:	Place:
Death Date:	Place:

Name:	(Wife) N°:
Marriage Date:	
Marriage Place:	
Nationality:	
Birth Date:	Place:
Death Date:	Place:
Citing this Record:	

Name:	N°:
Event Type-Draft Registration	
Event Date:	
Event Place:	
Nationality:	
Birth Date:	Place:
Death Date:	Place:

Name:	(Wife) N°:
Marriage Date:	
Marriage Place:	
Nationality:	
Birth Date:	Place:
Death Date:	Place:
Citing this Record:	

Name:	N°:
Event Type-Draft Registration	
Event Date:	
Event Place:	
Nationality:	
Birth Date:	Place:
Death Date:	Place:

Name:	(Wife) N°:
Marriage Date:	
Marriage Place:	
Nationality:	
Birth Date:	Place:
Death Date:	Place:
Citing this Record:	

SOURCES

Name: N°:

Event Type-Draft Registration
Event Date:
Event Place:
Nationality:

Birth Date:	Place:
Death Date:	Place:

Name: (Wife) N°:

Marriage Date:
Marriage Place:
Nationality:

Birth Date:	Place:
Death Date:	Place:

Citing this Record:

Name: N°:

Event Type-Draft Registration
Event Date:
Event Place:
Nationality:

Birth Date:	Place:
Death Date:	Place:

Name: (Wife) N°:

Marriage Date:
Marriage Place:
Nationality:

Birth Date:	Place:
Death Date:	Place:

Citing this Record:

Name: N°:

Event Type-Draft Registration
Event Date:
Event Place:
Nationality:

Birth Date:	Place:
Death Date:	Place:

Name: (Wife) N°:

Marriage Date:
Marriage Place:
Nationality:

Birth Date:	Place:
Death Date:	Place:

Citing this Record:

Name: N°:

Event Type-Draft Registration
Event Date:
Event Place:
Nationality:

Birth Date:	Place:
Death Date:	Place:

Name: (Wife) N°:

Marriage Date:
Marriage Place:
Nationality:

Birth Date:	Place:
Death Date:	Place:

Citing this Record:

SOURCES

Name: N°:	**Name:** (Wife) N°:
Event Type-Draft Registration	Marriage Date:
Event Date:	Marriage Place:
Event Place:	**Nationality:**
	Birth Date: | Place:
Nationality:	Death Date: | Place:
Birth Date: | Place:	Citing this Record:
Death Date: | Place:	

Name: N°:	**Name:** (Wife) N°:
Event Type-Draft Registration	Marriage Date:
Event Date:	Marriage Place:
Event Place:	**Nationality:**
	Birth Date: | Place:
Nationality:	Death Date: | Place:
Birth Date: | Place:	Citing this Record:
Death Date: | Place:	

Name: N°:	**Name:** (Wife) N°:
Event Type-Draft Registration	Marriage Date:
Event Date:	Marriage Place:
Event Place:	**Nationality:**
	Birth Date: | Place:
Nationality:	Death Date: | Place:
Birth Date: | Place:	Citing this Record:
Death Date: | Place:	

Name: N°:	**Name:** (Wife) N°:
Event Type-Draft Registration	Marriage Date:
Event Date:	Marriage Place:
Event Place:	**Nationality:**
	Birth Date: | Place:
Nationality:	Death Date: | Place:
Birth Date: | Place:	Citing this Record:
Death Date: | Place:	

SOURCES

Name:	N°:
Event Type-Draft Registration	
Event Date:	
Event Place:	
Nationality:	
Birth Date:	Place:
Death Date:	Place:

Name:	(Wife) N°:
Marriage Date:	
Marriage Place:	
Nationality:	
Birth Date:	Place:
Death Date:	Place:
Citing this Record:	

Name:	N°:
Event Type-Draft Registration	
Event Date:	
Event Place:	
Nationality:	
Birth Date:	Place:
Death Date:	Place:

Name:	(Wife) N°:
Marriage Date:	
Marriage Place:	
Nationality:	
Birth Date:	Place:
Death Date:	Place:
Citing this Record:	

Name:	N°:
Event Type-Draft Registration	
Event Date:	
Event Place:	
Nationality:	
Birth Date:	Place:
Death Date:	Place:

Name:	(Wife) N°:
Marriage Date:	
Marriage Place:	
Nationality:	
Birth Date:	Place:
Death Date:	Place:
Citing this Record:	

Name:	N°:
Event Type-Draft Registration	
Event Date:	
Event Place:	
Nationality:	
Birth Date:	Place:
Death Date:	Place:

Name:	(Wife) N°:
Marriage Date:	
Marriage Place:	
Nationality:	
Birth Date:	Place:
Death Date:	Place:
Citing this Record:	

SOURCES

Name: N°:

Event Type-Draft Registration	
Event Date:	
Event Place:	
Nationality:	
Birth Date:	Place:
Death Date:	Place:

Name: (Wife)   N°:

Marriage Date:	
Marriage Place:	
Nationality:	
Birth Date:	Place:
Death Date:	Place:
Citing this Record:	

Name: N°:

Event Type-Draft Registration	
Event Date:	
Event Place:	
Nationality:	
Birth Date:	Place:
Death Date:	Place:

Name: (Wife)   N°:

Marriage Date:	
Marriage Place:	
Nationality:	
Birth Date:	Place:
Death Date:	Place:
Citing this Record:	

Name: N°:

Event Type-Draft Registration	
Event Date:	
Event Place:	
Nationality:	
Birth Date:	Place:
Death Date:	Place:

Name: (Wife)   N°:

Marriage Date:	
Marriage Place:	
Nationality:	
Birth Date:	Place:
Death Date:	Place:
Citing this Record:	

Name: N°:

Event Type-Draft Registration	
Event Date:	
Event Place:	
Nationality:	
Birth Date:	Place:
Death Date:	Place:

Name: (Wife)   N°:

Marriage Date:	
Marriage Place:	
Nationality:	
Birth Date:	Place:
Death Date:	Place:
Citing this Record:	

SOURCES

Name:	N°:
Event Type-Draft Registration	
Event Date:	
Event Place:	
Nationality:	
Birth Date:	Place:
Death Date:	Place:

Name:	(Wife)	N°:
Marriage Date:		
Marriage Place:		
Nationality:		
Birth Date:	Place:	
Death Date:	Place:	
Citing this Record:		

Name:	N°:
Event Type-Draft Registration	
Event Date:	
Event Place:	
Nationality:	
Birth Date:	Place:
Death Date:	Place:

Name:	(Wife)	N°:
Marriage Date:		
Marriage Place:		
Nationality:		
Birth Date:	Place:	
Death Date:	Place:	
Citing this Record:		

Name:	N°:
Event Type-Draft Registration	
Event Date:	
Event Place:	
Nationality:	
Birth Date:	Place:
Death Date:	Place:

Name:	(Wife)	N°:
Marriage Date:		
Marriage Place:		
Nationality:		
Birth Date:	Place:	
Death Date:	Place:	
Citing this Record:		

Name:	N°:
Event Type-Draft Registration	
Event Date:	
Event Place:	
Nationality:	
Birth Date:	Place:
Death Date:	Place:

Name:	(Wife)	N°:
Marriage Date:		
Marriage Place:		
Nationality:		
Birth Date:	Place:	
Death Date:	Place:	
Citing this Record:		

SOURCES

Name:	N°:
Event Type-Draft Registration	
Event Date:	
Event Place:	
Nationality:	
Birth Date:	Place:
Death Date:	Place:

Name:	(Wife) N°:
Marriage Date:	
Marriage Place:	
Nationality:	
Birth Date:	Place:
Death Date:	Place:
Citing this Record:	

Name:	N°:
Event Type-Draft Registration	
Event Date:	
Event Place:	
Nationality:	
Birth Date:	Place:
Death Date:	Place:

Name:	(Wife) N°:
Marriage Date:	
Marriage Place:	
Nationality:	
Birth Date:	Place:
Death Date:	Place:
Citing this Record:	

Name:	N°:
Event Type-Draft Registration	
Event Date:	
Event Place:	
Nationality:	
Birth Date:	Place:
Death Date:	Place:

Name:	(Wife) N°:
Marriage Date:	
Marriage Place:	
Nationality:	
Birth Date:	Place:
Death Date:	Place:
Citing this Record:	

Name:	N°:
Event Type-Draft Registration	
Event Date:	
Event Place:	
Nationality:	
Birth Date:	Place:
Death Date:	Place:

Name:	(Wife) N°:
Marriage Date:	
Marriage Place:	
Nationality:	
Birth Date:	Place:
Death Date:	Place:
Citing this Record:	

SOURCES _____

Name:	N°:
Event Type-Draft Registration	
Event Date:	
Event Place:	
Nationality:	
Birth Date:	Place:
Death Date:	Place:

Name:	(Wife)	N°:
Marriage Date:		
Marriage Place:		
Nationality:		
Birth Date:	Place:	
Death Date:	Place:	
Citing this Record:		

Name:	N°:
Event Type-Draft Registration	
Event Date:	
Event Place:	
Nationality:	
Birth Date:	Place:
Death Date:	Place:

Name:	(Wife)	N°:
Marriage Date:		
Marriage Place:		
Nationality:		
Birth Date:	Place:	
Death Date:	Place:	
Citing this Record:		

Name:	N°:
Event Type-Draft Registration	
Event Date:	
Event Place:	
Nationality:	
Birth Date:	Place:
Death Date:	Place:

Name:	(Wife)	N°:
Marriage Date:		
Marriage Place:		
Nationality:		
Birth Date:	Place:	
Death Date:	Place:	
Citing this Record:		

Name:	N°:
Event Type-Draft Registration	
Event Date:	
Event Place:	
Nationality:	
Birth Date:	Place:
Death Date:	Place:

Name:	(Wife)	N°:
Marriage Date:		
Marriage Place:		
Nationality:		
Birth Date:	Place:	
Death Date:	Place:	
Citing this Record:		

SOURCES

Name:	N°:
Event Type-Draft Registration	
Event Date:	
Event Place:	
Nationality:	
Birth Date:	Place:
Death Date:	Place:

Name:	(Wife) N°:
Marriage Date:	
Marriage Place:	
Nationality:	
Birth Date:	Place:
Death Date:	Place:
Citing this Record:	

Name:	N°:
Event Type-Draft Registration	
Event Date:	
Event Place:	
Nationality:	
Birth Date:	Place:
Death Date:	Place:

Name:	(Wife) N°:
Marriage Date:	
Marriage Place:	
Nationality:	
Birth Date:	Place:
Death Date:	Place:
Citing this Record:	

Name:	N°:
Event Type-Draft Registration	
Event Date:	
Event Place:	
Nationality:	
Birth Date:	Place:
Death Date:	Place:

Name:	(Wife) N°:
Marriage Date:	
Marriage Place:	
Nationality:	
Birth Date:	Place:
Death Date:	Place:
Citing this Record:	

Name:	N°:
Event Type-Draft Registration	
Event Date:	
Event Place:	
Nationality:	
Birth Date:	Place:
Death Date:	Place:

Name:	(Wife) N°:
Marriage Date:	
Marriage Place:	
Nationality:	
Birth Date:	Place:
Death Date:	Place:
Citing this Record:	

SOURCES

Name:	N°:
Event Type-Draft Registration	
Event Date:	
Event Place:	
Nationality:	
Birth Date:	Place:
Death Date:	Place:

Name:	(Wife) N°:
Marriage Date:	
Marriage Place:	
Nationality:	
Birth Date:	Place:
Death Date:	Place:
Citing this Record:	

Name:	N°:
Event Type-Draft Registration	
Event Date:	
Event Place:	
Nationality:	
Birth Date:	Place:
Death Date:	Place:

Name:	(Wife) N°:
Marriage Date:	
Marriage Place:	
Nationality:	
Birth Date:	Place:
Death Date:	Place:
Citing this Record:	

Name:	N°:
Event Type-Draft Registration	
Event Date:	
Event Place:	
Nationality:	
Birth Date:	Place:
Death Date:	Place:

Name:	(Wife) N°:
Marriage Date:	
Marriage Place:	
Nationality:	
Birth Date:	Place:
Death Date:	Place:
Citing this Record:	

Name:	N°:
Event Type-Draft Registration	
Event Date:	
Event Place:	
Nationality:	
Birth Date:	Place:
Death Date:	Place:

Name:	(Wife) N°:
Marriage Date:	
Marriage Place:	
Nationality:	
Birth Date:	Place:
Death Date:	Place:
Citing this Record:	

STORIES

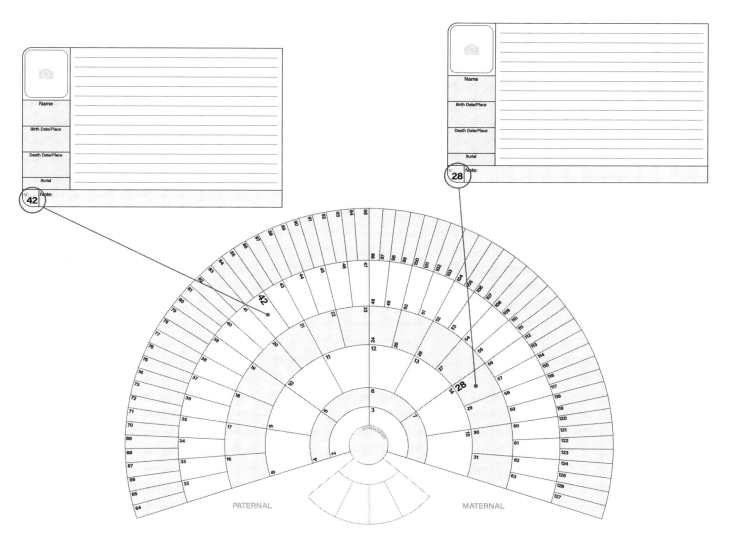

The Stories FAN CHART clarification each box according to how many stories or memories have been you recordit and attached to each person in the chart.

This view makes it easy to see which family members have stories read about.

STORIES

Compiled By: _____

Date: _____

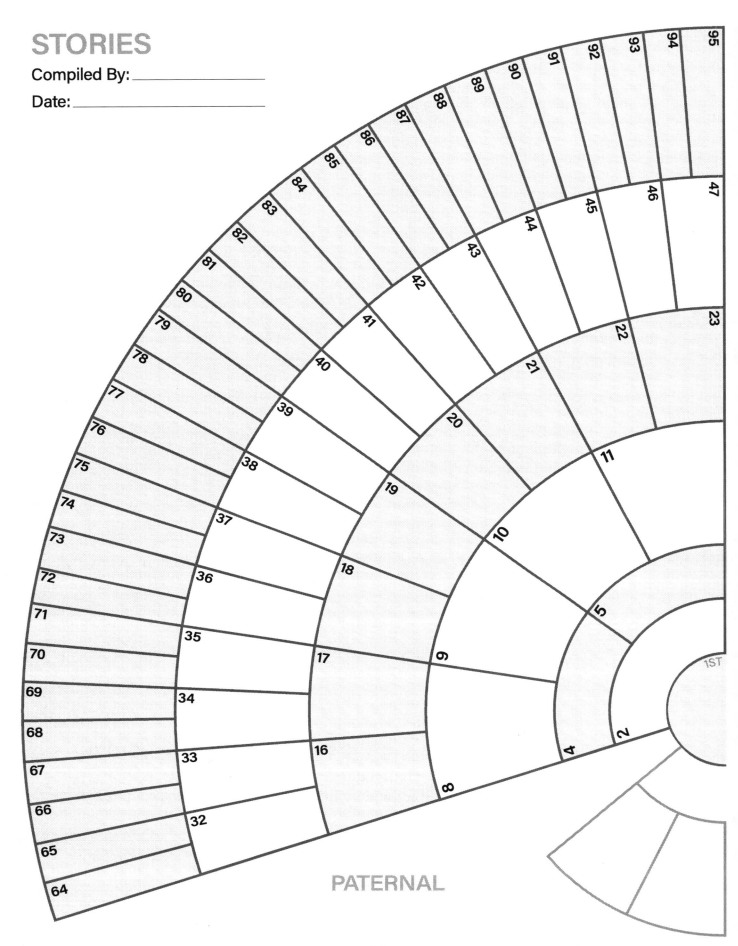

PATERNAL

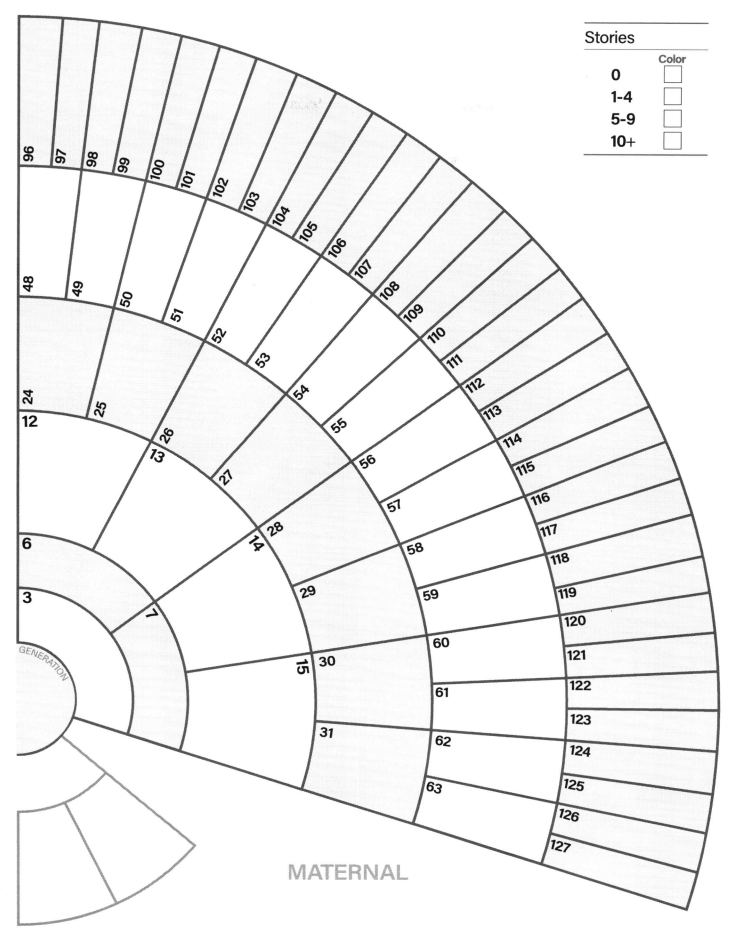

Color

0

1-4

5-9

10+

GENERATION

MATERNAL

35

Name
Birth Date/Place
Death Date/Place
Burial

N°: | Note:

Name
Birth Date/Place
Death Date/Place
Burial

N°: | Note:

	Name
	Birth Date/Place
	Death Date/Place
	Burial

N°: | Note:

	Name
	Birth Date/Place
	Death Date/Place
	Burial

N°: | Note:

STORIES

📷	
Name	
Birth Date/Place	
Death Date/Place	
Burial	
N°:	**Note:**

📷	
Name	
Birth Date/Place	
Death Date/Place	
Burial	
N°:	**Note:**

Name

Birth Date/Place

Death Date/Place

Burial

N°: **Note:**

Name

Birth Date/Place

Death Date/Place

Burial

N°: **Note:**

Name

Birth Date/Place

Death Date/Place

Burial

N°: Note:

Name

Birth Date/Place

Death Date/Place

Burial

N°: Note:

Name	
Birth Date/Place	
Death Date/Place	
Burial	

N°: **Note:**

Name	
Birth Date/Place	
Death Date/Place	
Burial	

N°: **Note:**

Name

Birth Date/Place

Death Date/Place

Burial

Nº: Note:

Name

Birth Date/Place

Death Date/Place

Burial

Nº: Note:

Name

Birth Date/Place

Death Date/Place

Burial

N°: Note:

Name

Birth Date/Place

Death Date/Place

Burial

N°: Note:

Name

Birth Date/Place

Death Date/Place

Burial

N°:   Note:

Name

Birth Date/Place

Death Date/Place

Burial

N°:   Note:

Name	
Birth Date/Place	
Death Date/Place	
Burial	

N°: **Note:**

Name	
Birth Date/Place	
Death Date/Place	
Burial	

N°: **Note:**

Name	
Birth Date/Place	
Death Date/Place	
Burial	
N°:	Note:

Name	
Birth Date/Place	
Death Date/Place	
Burial	
N°:	Note:

STORIES

Name	
Birth Date/Place	
Death Date/Place	
Burial	

N°: Note:

Name	
Birth Date/Place	
Death Date/Place	
Burial	

N°: Note:

STORIES

Name

Birth Date/Place

Death Date/Place

Burial

N°: | Note:

Name

Birth Date/Place

Death Date/Place

Burial

N°: | Note:

Name

Birth Date/Place

Death Date/Place

Burial

Nº: Note:

Name

Birth Date/Place

Death Date/Place

Burial

Nº: Note:

STORIES

Name

Birth Date/Place

Death Date/Place

Burial

N°:   Note:

Name

Birth Date/Place

Death Date/Place

Burial

N°:   Note:

Name
Birth Date/Place
Death Date/Place
Burial

N°: Note:

Name
Birth Date/Place
Death Date/Place
Burial

N°: Note:

[camera icon]	
Name	
Birth Date/Place	
Death Date/Place	
Burial	
N°:	**Note:**

[camera icon]	
Name	
Birth Date/Place	
Death Date/Place	
Burial	
N°:	**Note:**

Name	
Birth Date/Place	
Death Date/Place	
Burial	

N°: **Note:**

Name	
Birth Date/Place	
Death Date/Place	
Burial	

N°: **Note:**

STORIES

Name	
Birth Date/Place	
Death Date/Place	
Burial	

N°: **Note:**

Name	
Birth Date/Place	
Death Date/Place	
Burial	

N°: **Note:**

Name	
Birth Date/Place	
Death Date/Place	
Burial	
N°:	**Note:**

Name	
Birth Date/Place	
Death Date/Place	
Burial	
N°:	**Note:**

STORIES

Name

Birth Date/Place

Death Date/Place

Burial

N°: Note:

Name

Birth Date/Place

Death Date/Place

Burial

N°: Note:

STORIES

📷	
Name	
Birth Date/Place	
Death Date/Place	
Burial	

N°:   **Note:**

📷	
Name	
Birth Date/Place	
Death Date/Place	
Burial	

N°:   **Note:**

STORIES

Name

Birth Date/Place

Death Date/Place

Burial

N°: **Note:**

Name

Birth Date/Place

Death Date/Place

Burial

N°: **Note:**

STORIES

Name
Birth Date/Place
Death Date/Place
Burial

N°: **Note:**

Name
Birth Date/Place
Death Date/Place
Burial

N°: **Note:**

Name	
Birth Date/Place	
Death Date/Place	
Burial	

N°:   Note:

Name	
Birth Date/Place	
Death Date/Place	
Burial	

N°:   Note:

STORIES

📷	
Name	
Birth Date/Place	
Death Date/Place	
Burial	
N°:	Note:

📷	
Name	
Birth Date/Place	
Death Date/Place	
Burial	
N°:	Note:

Name

Birth Date/Place

Death Date/Place

Burial

N°: Note:

Name

Birth Date/Place

Death Date/Place

Burial

N°: Note:

STORIES

Name
Birth Date/Place
Death Date/Place
Burial

N°:   Note:

Name
Birth Date/Place
Death Date/Place
Burial

N°:   Note:

Name
Birth Date/Place
Death Date/Place
Burial

N°: Note:

Name
Birth Date/Place
Death Date/Place
Burial

N°: Note:

STORIES

📷	
Name	
Birth Date/Place	
Death Date/Place	
Burial	
N°:	Note:

📷	
Name	
Birth Date/Place	
Death Date/Place	
Burial	
N°:	Note:

STORIES

Name	
Birth Date/Place	
Death Date/Place	
Burial	

N°: Note:

Name	
Birth Date/Place	
Death Date/Place	
Burial	

N°: Note:

STORIES

Name	
Birth Date/Place	
Death Date/Place	
Burial	

N°: Note:

Name	
Birth Date/Place	
Death Date/Place	
Burial	

N°: Note:

Name
Birth Date/Place
Death Date/Place
Burial

N°:   Note:

Name
Birth Date/Place
Death Date/Place
Burial

N°:   Note:

STORIES

📷	
Name	
Birth Date/Place	
Death Date/Place	
Burial	
N°:	**Note:**

📷	
Name	
Birth Date/Place	
Death Date/Place	
Burial	
N°:	**Note:**

Name	
Birth Date/Place	
Death Date/Place	
Burial	

Nº: Note:

Name	
Birth Date/Place	
Death Date/Place	
Burial	

Nº: Note:

STORIES

[camera icon]	
Name	
Birth Date/Place	
Death Date/Place	
Burial	

N°: **Note:**

[camera icon]	
Name	
Birth Date/Place	
Death Date/Place	
Burial	

N°: **Note:**

Name

Birth Date/Place

Death Date/Place

Burial

N°: Note:

Name

Birth Date/Place

Death Date/Place

Burial

N°: Note:

STORIES

Name

Birth Date/Place

Death Date/Place

Burial

N°: Note:

Name

Birth Date/Place

Death Date/Place

Burial

N°: Note:

74

STORIES

Name

Birth Date/Place

Death Date/Place

Burial

N°: Note:

Name

Birth Date/Place

Death Date/Place

Burial

N°: Note:

Name

Birth Date/Place

Death Date/Place

Burial

N°: Note:

Name

Birth Date/Place

Death Date/Place

Burial

N°: Note:

Name

Birth Date/Place

Death Date/Place

Burial

N°:   Note:

Name

Birth Date/Place

Death Date/Place

Burial

N°:   Note:

RESEARCH HELPS

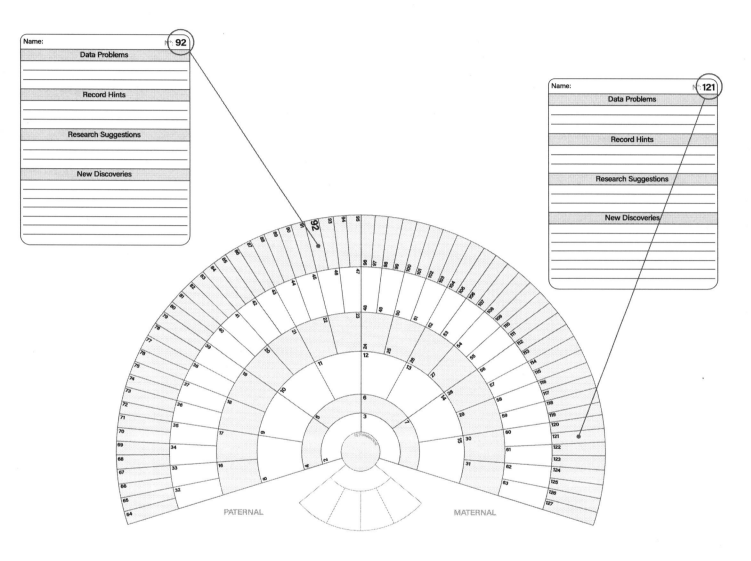

Name: _____ N°. **92**

Data Problems
_____
_____

Record Hints
_____
_____

Research Suggestions
_____
_____

New Discoveries
_____
_____
_____
_____
_____

Name: _____ N°. **121**

Data Problems
_____
_____

Record Hints
_____
_____

Research Suggestions
_____
_____

New Discoveries
_____
_____
_____
_____
_____

PATERNAL   MATERNAL

The Research Helps view of the genealogy chart can show you which people in your family tree could use a little more research.

Organize The boxes into three categories, each with its own color -Data Problems, Record Hints, and Research Suggestions.

RESEARCH HELPS

Compiled By: _____

Date: _____

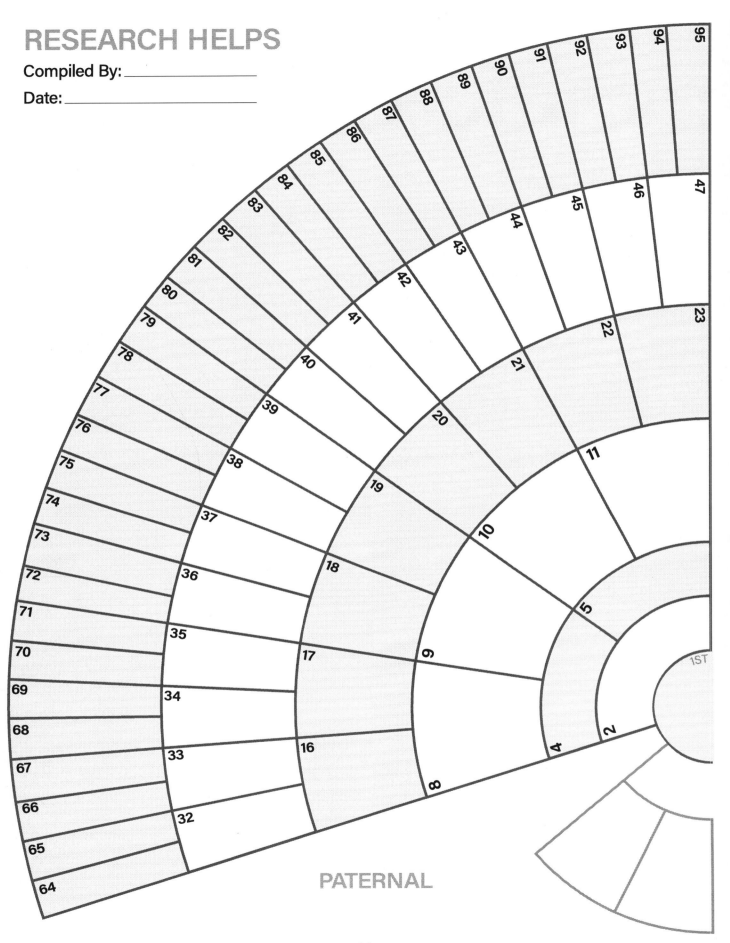

PATERNAL

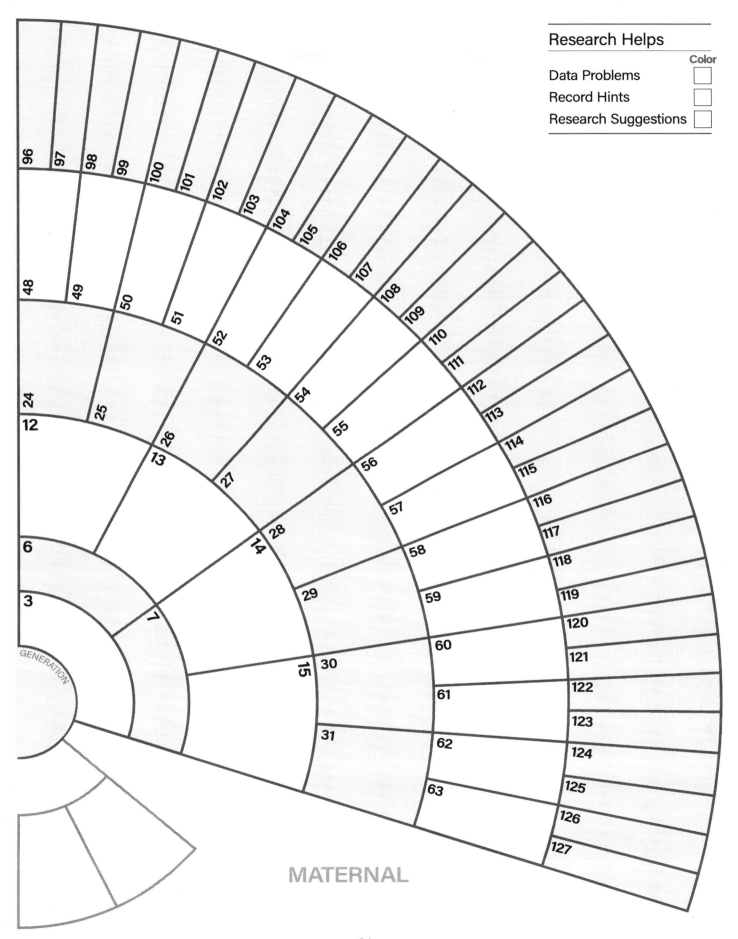

Color

Data Problems

Record Hints

Research Suggestions

96
97
98
99
100
101
102
103
104
105
106
107
108
109
110
111
112
113
114
115
116
117
118
119
120
121
122
123
124
125
126
127

48
49
50
51
52
53
54
55
56
57
58
59
60
61
62
63

24
25
26
27
28
29
30
31

12
13
14
15

6
7

3

GENERATION

MATERNAL

Name: N°:

Data Problems

Record Hints

Research Suggestions

New Discoveries

Name: N°:

Data Problems

Record Hints

Research Suggestions

New Discoveries

Name: N°:

Data Problems

Record Hints

Research Suggestions

New Discoveries

Name: N°:

Data Problems

Record Hints

Research Suggestions

New Discoveries

RESEARCH HELPS

Name: N°:

Data Problems

Record Hints

Research Suggestions

New Discoveries

Name: N°:

Data Problems

Record Hints

Research Suggestions

New Discoveries

Name: N°:

Data Problems

Record Hints

Research Suggestions

New Discoveries

Name: N°:

Data Problems

Record Hints

Research Suggestions

New Discoveries

RESEARCH HELPS

Name: _____ N°:

Data Problems

Record Hints

Research Suggestions

New Discoveries

Name: _____ N°:

Data Problems

Record Hints

Research Suggestions

New Discoveries

Name: _____ N°:

Data Problems

Record Hints

Research Suggestions

New Discoveries

Name: _____ N°:

Data Problems

Record Hints

Research Suggestions

New Discoveries

RESEARCH HELPS

Name: N°:

Data Problems

Record Hints

Research Suggestions

New Discoveries

Name: N°:

Data Problems

Record Hints

Research Suggestions

New Discoveries

Name: N°:

Data Problems

Record Hints

Research Suggestions

New Discoveries

Name: N°:

Data Problems

Record Hints

Research Suggestions

New Discoveries

Name: _____ N°: ___

Data Problems

Record Hints

Research Suggestions

New Discoveries

Name: _____ N°: ___

Data Problems

Record Hints

Research Suggestions

New Discoveries

Name: _____ N°: ___

Data Problems

Record Hints

Research Suggestions

New Discoveries

Name: _____ N°: ___

Data Problems

Record Hints

Research Suggestions

New Discoveries

RESEARCH HELPS

Name: N°:

Data Problems

Record Hints

Research Suggestions

New Discoveries

Name: N°:

Data Problems

Record Hints

Research Suggestions

New Discoveries

Name: N°:

Data Problems

Record Hints

Research Suggestions

New Discoveries

Name: N°:

Data Problems

Record Hints

Research Suggestions

New Discoveries

Name: _____ N°:

Data Problems

Record Hints

Research Suggestions

New Discoveries

Name: _____ N°:

Data Problems

Record Hints

Research Suggestions

New Discoveries

Name: _____ N°:

Data Problems

Record Hints

Research Suggestions

New Discoveries

Name: _____ N°:

Data Problems

Record Hints

Research Suggestions

New Discoveries

RESEARCH HELPS

Name: N°:

Data Problems

Record Hints

Research Suggestions

New Discoveries

Name: N°:

Data Problems

Record Hints

Research Suggestions

New Discoveries

Name: N°:

Data Problems

Record Hints

Research Suggestions

New Discoveries

Name: N°:

Data Problems

Record Hints

Research Suggestions

New Discoveries

RESEARCH HELPS

Name: N°:

Data Problems

Record Hints

Research Suggestions

New Discoveries

Name: N°:

Data Problems

Record Hints

Research Suggestions

New Discoveries

Name: N°:

Data Problems

Record Hints

Research Suggestions

New Discoveries

Name: N°:

Data Problems

Record Hints

Research Suggestions

New Discoveries

RESEARCH HELPS

Name: N°:

Data Problems

Record Hints

Research Suggestions

New Discoveries

Name: N°:

Data Problems

Record Hints

Research Suggestions

New Discoveries

Name: N°:

Data Problems

Record Hints

Research Suggestions

New Discoveries

Name: N°:

Data Problems

Record Hints

Research Suggestions

New Discoveries

RESEARCH HELPS

Name: _____ N°: ___

Data Problems

Record Hints

Research Suggestions

New Discoveries

Name: _____ N°: ___

Data Problems

Record Hints

Research Suggestions

New Discoveries

Name: _____ N°: ___

Data Problems

Record Hints

Research Suggestions

New Discoveries

Name: _____ N°: ___

Data Problems

Record Hints

Research Suggestions

New Discoveries

RESEARCH HELPS

Name: N°:

Data Problems

Record Hints

Research Suggestions

New Discoveries

Name: N°:

Data Problems

Record Hints

Research Suggestions

New Discoveries

Name: N°:

Data Problems

Record Hints

Research Suggestions

New Discoveries

Name: N°:

Data Problems

Record Hints

Research Suggestions

New Discoveries

RESEARCH HELPS

Name: _____ N°:

Data Problems

Record Hints

Research Suggestions

New Discoveries

Name: _____ N°:

Data Problems

Record Hints

Research Suggestions

New Discoveries

Name: _____ N°:

Data Problems

Record Hints

Research Suggestions

New Discoveries

Name: _____ N°:

Data Problems

Record Hints

Research Suggestions

New Discoveries

RESEARCH HELPS

Name: _____ N°:

Data Problems

Record Hints

Research Suggestions

New Discoveries

Name: _____ N°:

Data Problems

Record Hints

Research Suggestions

New Discoveries

Name: _____ N°:

Data Problems

Record Hints

Research Suggestions

New Discoveries

Name: _____ N°:

Data Problems

Record Hints

Research Suggestions

New Discoveries

Name: N°:

Data Problems

Record Hints

Research Suggestions

New Discoveries

Name: N°:

Data Problems

Record Hints

Research Suggestions

New Discoveries

Name: N°:

Data Problems

Record Hints

Research Suggestions

New Discoveries

Name: N°:

Data Problems

Record Hints

Research Suggestions

New Discoveries

RESEARCH HELPS

Name: _____ N°:

Data Problems

Record Hints

Research Suggestions

New Discoveries

Name: _____ N°:

Data Problems

Record Hints

Research Suggestions

New Discoveries

Name: _____ N°:

Data Problems

Record Hints

Research Suggestions

New Discoveries

Name: _____ N°:

Data Problems

Record Hints

Research Suggestions

New Discoveries

RESEARCH HELPS

Name: _____ N°:

Data Problems

Record Hints

Research Suggestions

New Discoveries

Name: _____ N°:

Data Problems

Record Hints

Research Suggestions

New Discoveries

Name: _____ N°:

Data Problems

Record Hints

Research Suggestions

New Discoveries

Name: _____ N°:

Data Problems

Record Hints

Research Suggestions

New Discoveries

RESEARCH HELPS

Name: N°:

Data Problems

Record Hints

Research Suggestions

New Discoveries

Name: N°:

Data Problems

Record Hints

Research Suggestions

New Discoveries

Name: N°:

Data Problems

Record Hints

Research Suggestions

New Discoveries

Name: N°:

Data Problems

Record Hints

Research Suggestions

New Discoveries

RESEARCH HELPS

Name: N°:

Data Problems

Record Hints

Research Suggestions

New Discoveries

Name: N°:

Data Problems

Record Hints

Research Suggestions

New Discoveries

Name: N°:

Data Problems

Record Hints

Research Suggestions

New Discoveries

Name: N°:

Data Problems

Record Hints

Research Suggestions

New Discoveries

RESEARCH HELPS

Name: N°:

Data Problems

Record Hints

Research Suggestions

New Discoveries

Name: N°:

Data Problems

Record Hints

Research Suggestions

New Discoveries

Name: N°:

Data Problems

Record Hints

Research Suggestions

New Discoveries

Name: N°:

Data Problems

Record Hints

Research Suggestions

New Discoveries

RESEARCH HELPS

Name: N°:

Data Problems

Record Hints

Research Suggestions

New Discoveries

Name: N°:

Data Problems

Record Hints

Research Suggestions

New Discoveries

Name: N°:

Data Problems

Record Hints

Research Suggestions

New Discoveries

Name: N°:

Data Problems

Record Hints

Research Suggestions

New Discoveries

RESEARCH HELPS

Name: _____ N°:

Data Problems

Record Hints

Research Suggestions

New Discoveries

Name: _____ N°:

Data Problems

Record Hints

Research Suggestions

New Discoveries

Name: _____ N°:

Data Problems

Record Hints

Research Suggestions

New Discoveries

Name: _____ N°:

Data Problems

Record Hints

Research Suggestions

New Discoveries

RESEARCH HELPS

Name: N°:

Data Problems

Record Hints

Research Suggestions

New Discoveries

Name: N°:

Data Problems

Record Hints

Research Suggestions

New Discoveries

Name: N°:

Data Problems

Record Hints

Research Suggestions

New Discoveries

Name: N°:

Data Problems

Record Hints

Research Suggestions

New Discoveries

RESEARCH HELPS

Name: N°:

Data Problems

Record Hints

Research Suggestions

New Discoveries

Name: N°:

Data Problems

Record Hints

Research Suggestions

New Discoveries

Name: N°:

Data Problems

Record Hints

Research Suggestions

New Discoveries

Name: N°:

Data Problems

Record Hints

Research Suggestions

New Discoveries

RESEARCH HELPS

Name: _____ N°:

Data Problems

Record Hints

Research Suggestions

New Discoveries

Name: _____ N°:

Data Problems

Record Hints

Research Suggestions

New Discoveries

Name: _____ N°:

Data Problems

Record Hints

Research Suggestions

New Discoveries

Name: _____ N°:

Data Problems

Record Hints

Research Suggestions

New Discoveries

RESEARCH HELPS

Name: Nº:

Data Problems

Record Hints

Research Suggestions

New Discoveries

Name: Nº:

Data Problems

Record Hints

Research Suggestions

New Discoveries

Name: Nº:

Data Problems

Record Hints

Research Suggestions

New Discoveries

Name: Nº:

Data Problems

Record Hints

Research Suggestions

New Discoveries

Name: _____ N°: _____

Data Problems
_____
_____
_____

Record Hints
_____
_____
_____

Research Suggestions
_____
_____
_____

New Discoveries
_____
_____
_____
_____
_____
_____
_____

Name: _____ N°: _____

Data Problems
_____
_____
_____

Record Hints
_____
_____
_____

Research Suggestions
_____
_____
_____

New Discoveries
_____
_____
_____
_____
_____
_____
_____

Name: _____ N°: _____

Data Problems
_____
_____
_____

Record Hints
_____
_____
_____

Research Suggestions
_____
_____
_____

New Discoveries
_____
_____
_____
_____
_____
_____
_____

Name: _____ N°: _____

Data Problems
_____
_____
_____

Record Hints
_____
_____
_____

Research Suggestions
_____
_____
_____

New Discoveries
_____
_____
_____
_____
_____
_____
_____

RESEARCH HELPS

Name: N°:

Data Problems

Record Hints

Research Suggestions

New Discoveries

Name: N°:

Data Problems

Record Hints

Research Suggestions

New Discoveries

Name: N°:

Data Problems

Record Hints

Research Suggestions

New Discoveries

Name: N°:

Data Problems

Record Hints

Research Suggestions

New Discoveries

RESEARCH HELPS

Name: N°:

Data Problems

Record Hints

Research Suggestions

New Discoveries

Name: N°:

Data Problems

Record Hints

Research Suggestions

New Discoveries

Name: N°:

Data Problems

Record Hints

Research Suggestions

New Discoveries

Name: N°:

Data Problems

Record Hints

Research Suggestions

New Discoveries

RESEARCH HELPS

Name: N°:

Data Problems

Record Hints

Research Suggestions

New Discoveries

Name: N°:

Data Problems

Record Hints

Research Suggestions

New Discoveries

Name: N°:

Data Problems

Record Hints

Research Suggestions

New Discoveries

Name: N°:

Data Problems

Record Hints

Research Suggestions

New Discoveries

RESEARCH HELPS

Name: _____ N°:

Data Problems

Record Hints

Research Suggestions

New Discoveries

Name: _____ N°:

Data Problems

Record Hints

Research Suggestions

New Discoveries

Name: _____ N°:

Data Problems

Record Hints

Research Suggestions

New Discoveries

Name: _____ N°:

Data Problems

Record Hints

Research Suggestions

New Discoveries

FAMILY GROUP SHEET _____

Husband's full name: _____

	DATE	LOCATION	ADDITIONAL INFO
Born:			
Married:			
Died:			
Buried:			
Other Marriage:			

Husband's Father:	Husband's Mother:

ADDITIONAL NOTES:

Wife's full name: _____

	DATE	LOCATION	ADDITIONAL INFO
Born:			
Married:			
Died:			
Buried:			
Other Marriage:			

Husband's Father:	Husband's Mother:

ADDITIONAL NOTES:

1st Child: _____

Male: ☐ Female: ☐	DATE	LOCATION	ADDITIONAL INFO
Born:			
Married:			
Died:			
Spouse:			

Notes:

Prepared by / Date:

2nd Child: _____

Male: ☐ Female: ☐	DATE	LOCATION	ADDITIONAL INFO
Born:			
Married:			
Died:			
Spouse:			

3th Child: _____

Male: ☐ Female: ☐	DATE	LOCATION	ADDITIONAL INFO
Born:			
Married:			
Died:			
Spouse:			

4th Child: _____

Male: ☐ Female: ☐	DATE	LOCATION	ADDITIONAL INFO
Born:			
Married:			
Died:			
Spouse:			

5th Child: _____

Male: ☐ Female: ☐	DATE	LOCATION	ADDITIONAL INFO
Born:			
Married:			
Died:			
Spouse:			

Notes:

Prepared by / Date:

6th Child: _____

Male: ☐ Female: ☐	DATE	LOCATION	ADDITIONAL INFO
Born:			
Married:			
Died:			
Spouse:			

7th Child: _____

Male: ☐ Female: ☐	DATE	LOCATION	ADDITIONAL INFO
Born:			
Married:			
Died:			
Spouse:			

8th Child: _____

Male: ☐ Female: ☐	DATE	LOCATION	ADDITIONAL INFO
Born:			
Married:			
Died:			
Spouse:			

9th Child: _____

Male: ☐ Female: ☐	DATE	LOCATION	ADDITIONAL INFO
Born:			
Married:			
Died:			
Spouse:			

Notes:

Prepared by / Date:

SOURCES

Notes:

Prepared by / Date:

FAMILY RELATIONSHIP CHART

- On the top row, find the relationship of Person A to the common ancestor. Follow that column down.

- Next find the relationship of Person B to the common ancestor. Follow that row across.

- The relationship of Person A and Person B is found where the column and the row intersect.

- R means 'removed' ie first cousin twice removed.

FAMILY RELATIONSHIP CHART

Common Ancestor	Child	Grandchild	Great Grandchild	2nd Great Grandchild	3rd Great Grandchild	4th Great Grandchild	5th Great Grandchild	6th Great Grandchild	7th Great Grandchild
Child	Sibling	Niece/Nephew	Grandniece/Grandnephew	Great Grandniece/Grandnephew	2nd Great Grandniece/Grandnephew	3rd Great Grandniece/Grandnephew	4th Great Grandniece/Grandnephew	5th Great Grandniece/Grandnephew	6th Great Grandniece/Grandnephew
Grandchild	Niece/Nephew	First Cousin	First Cousin 1R	First Cousin 2R	First Cousin 3R	First Cousin 4R	First Cousin 5R	First Cousin 6R	First Cousin 7R
Great Grandchild	Grandniece/Grandnephew	First Cousin 1R	Second Cousin	Second Cousin 1R	Second Cousin 2R	Second Cousin 3R	Second Cousin 4R	Second Cousin 5R	Second Cousin 6R
2nd Great Grandchild	Great Grandniece/Grandnephew	First Cousin 2R	Second Cousin 1R	Third Cousin	Third Cousin 1R	Third Cousin 2R	Third Cousin 3R	Third Cousin 4R	Third Cousin 5R
3rd Great Grandchild	3rd Great Grandniece/Grandnephew	First Cousin 3R	Second Cousin 2R	Third Cousin 1R	Fourth Cousin	Fourth Cousin 1R	Fourth Cousin 2R	Fourth Cousin 3R	Fourth Cousin 4R
4th Great Grandchild	2nd Great Grandniece/Grandnephew	First Cousin 4R	Second Cousin 3R	Third Cousin 2R	Fourth Cousin 1R	Fifth Cousin	Fifth Cousin 1R	Fifth Cousin 2R	Fifth Cousin 3R
5th Great Grandchild	4th Great Grandniece/Grandnephew	First Cousin 5R	Second Cousin 4R	Third Cousin 3R	Fourth Cousin 2R	Fifth Cousin 1R	Sixth Cousin	Sixth Cousin 1R	Sixth Cousin 2R
6th Great Grandchild	5th Great Grandniece/Grandnephew	First Cousin 6R	Second Cousin 5R	Third Cousin 4R	Fourth Cousin 3R	Fifth Cousin 2R	Sixth Cousin 1R	Seventh Cousin	Seventh Cousin 1R
7th Great Grandchild	6th Great Grandniece/Grandnephew	First Cousin 7R	Second Cousin 6R	Third Cousin 5R	Fourth Cousin 4R	Fifth Cousin 3R	Sixth Cousin 2R	Seventh Cousin 1R	Eighth Cousin

Hi Dear

I'm so thrilled you've chosen to purchase Genealogy Organizer from me, I hope you love it! If you do, would you consider posting an online review on AMAZON! This helps me to continue providing great products! and helps potential buyers to make confident decisions,

Thank you in advance for your review, I wish you good luck in your life.

Daniel Mary

_____

93ace97e-ce69-4b7c-9629-f5765af64260R01